JUMBO COLORING & ACTIVITY BOOK

D0570632

© 2014 Bendon. All rights reserved.
The BENDON name, logo, and Tear and Share are trademarks of Bendon, Ashland, OH 44805.

HASBRO and its logo, MY LITTLE PONY and all related characters are trademarks of Hasbro and are used with permission.
© 2012 Hasbro.
All Rights Reserved.

MAKE A MATCH

Look at the 3 ponies in each column. Find the ponies that match and draw a line connecting the two.

TWILIGHT
SPARKLE

pony
pals

WHO IS WHO?

Draw a line from each pony's cutie mark to her correct name.

1 

2 

3 

A PRINCESS CELESTIA

B RAINBOW DASH

C FLUTTERSHY

Answer: 1 is C, 2 is B, 3 is A.

I Love
pinkie
pie

COLOR BY NUMBER

Use the key below
to color the picture.

1. blue 2. red 3. pink
4. yellow 5. green 6. orange

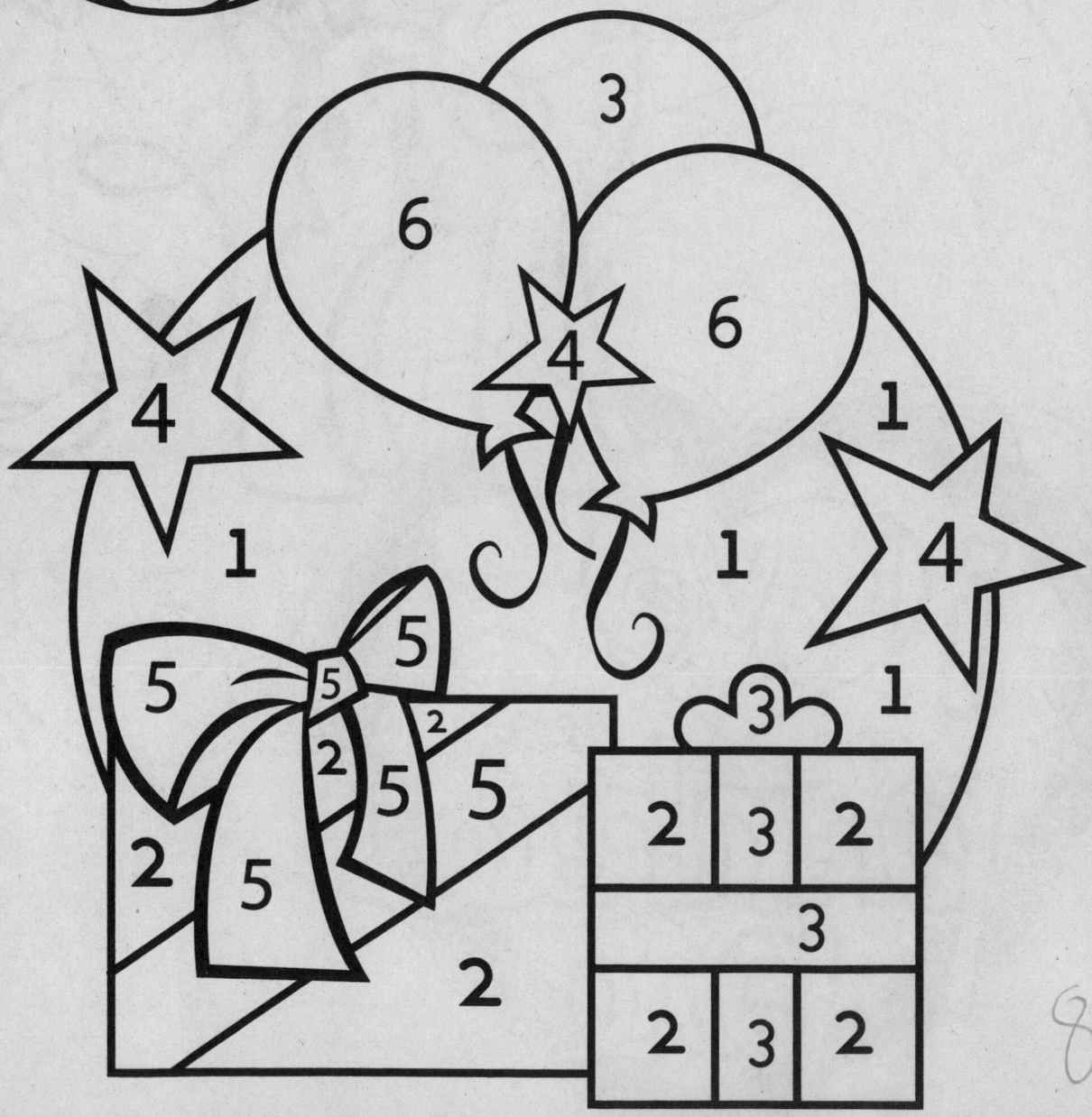

♡ princess celestia ♡

♡ princess celestia ♡

PONY MAZE

Help Princess Celestia fly to the sun and the moon.

RARITY

Find the star. Color it yellow.
Find the heart. Color it pink.
Find the diamond. Color it blue.
12

Rainbow Dash

PONY MAZE

Help Rainbow Dash fly to her friend Twilight Sparkle.

APPLEJACK

FUN FILL-INS

Fill in the missing letters to reveal each word below.

HINT: Applejack lives there:

S_W_EET AP_P_L_E

_?_CRES

Answer: SWEET APPLE ACRES.

FLUTTERSHY

HOW MANY?

Count the items below and place your answer on the line.

_____ BUTTERFLIES.

Answer: 8 Butterflies

Lil' Bit
COUNTRY

TWIN PONIES!

Can you find the two ponies that are exactly the same?

Answer: 2 and 3 are the same.

pony
pals

MAKE A MATCH

Look at the 3 ponies in each column. Find the ponies that match and draw a line connecting the two.

twilight
sparkle

LET'S DRAW!

Use the grid to help you draw a star.

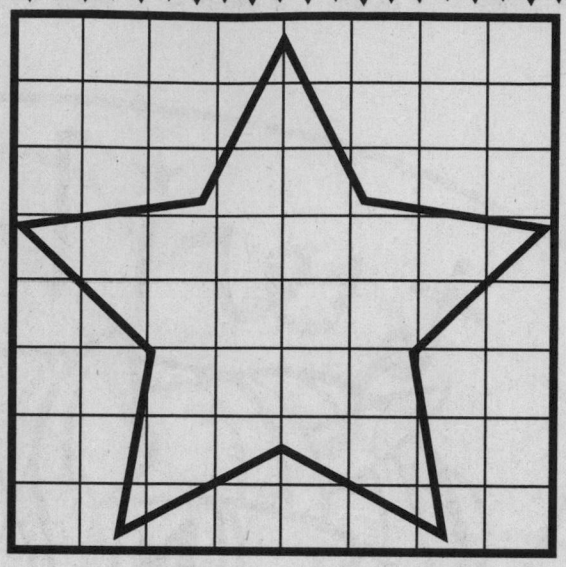

WHO IS WHO?

Draw a line from each pony's cutie mark to her correct name.

1 

A RARITY

2 

B APPLEJACK

3 

C TWILIGHT SPARKLE

Answer: 1 is C, 2 is B, 3 is A.

LET'S DRAW!

A trail of butterflies follows Fluttershy everywhere she goes. Draw some butterflies.

How 'bout them
APPLES?

COLOR BY NUMBER

Use the key below
to color the picture.

1. blue 2. green 3. red
4. yellow 5. pink

PONY MAZE

Follow the path of flowers to help the bunnies find their way to Fluttershy.

HOW MANY?

Count the items below and place your answer on the line.

_____ HEARTS.

Answer: 12 Hearts.

MAKE A MATCH

Look at the 3 ponies in each column. Find the ponies that match and draw a line connecting the two.

twilight
sparkle

PONY SQUARES

Taking turns, connect a line from one star to another. Whoever makes the line that completes a box puts their initial inside the box. The person with the most squares at the end of the game wins!

EXAMPLE

TWIN PONIES!

Can you find the two ponies that are exactly the same?

1.

2.

3.

4.

Answer: 1 and 4 are the same.

MY LITTLE PONY MIX-UP

Unscramble the words below.

ISNG

_____

UBTTERLFIES

_____

NGETLE

_____

Answers: Sing, Butterflies, Gentle.

FARM
F•R•E•S•H

CONNECT THE DOTS

Connect the dots by alphabetical order.

A B C D E F G H I J K L M N O P Q R S T U V W X Y Z

Rainbow Dash

FUN FILL-INS

Fill in the missing letters to reveal each word below.

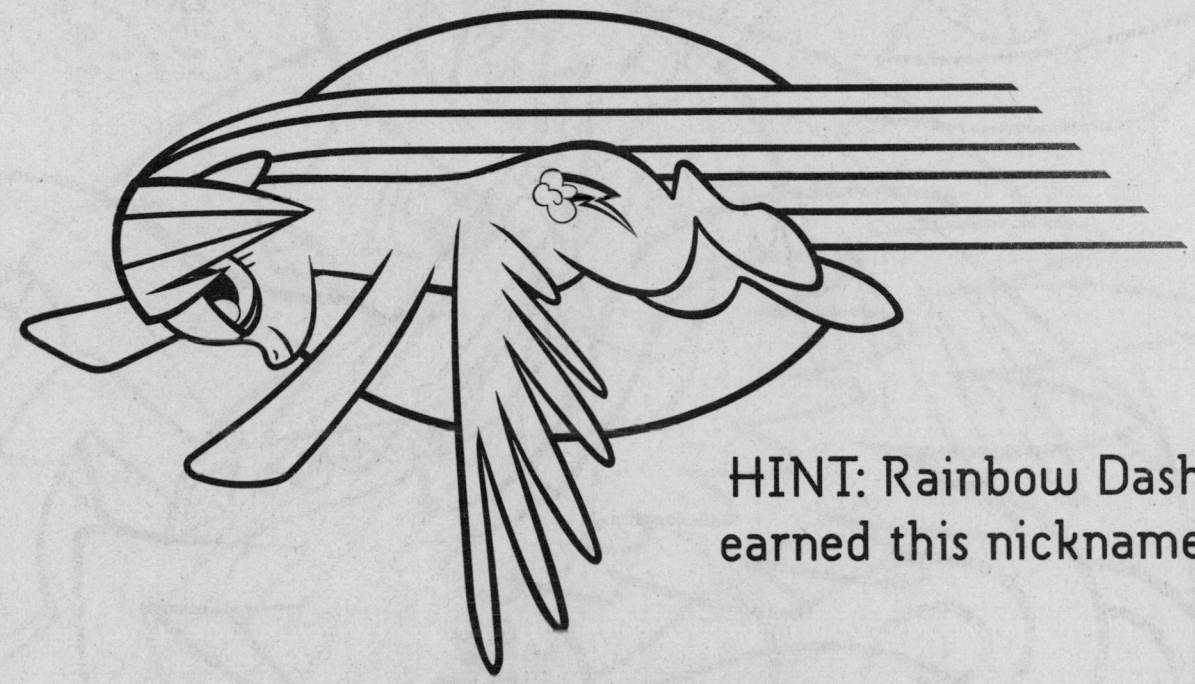

HINT: Rainbow Dash earned this nickname:

AINBO

_RASH

Answer: RAINBOW CRASH

princess celestia

princess celestia

LET'S DRAW!

Princess Celestia is the ruler of Equestria. Draw a sun and moon.

FLUTTERSHY

CONNECT THE DOTS
Connect the dots by alphabetical order.
A
B
C
D
E
F
G
H
I
J
K
L
M
N
O
P
Q
R
S
T
U
V
W
X
Y
Z

MY LITTLE PONY MIX-UP

Unscramble the words below.

EBAUYT

_____

PSARLKE

_____

OBUTIQEU

_____

Answers: Beauty, Sparkle, Boutique.

SPIKE
THE DRAGON

MAKE A MATCH

Look at the 3 ponies in each column. Find the ponies that match and draw a line connecting the two.

LET'S DRAW!

Use the grid to help you draw a diamond ring.

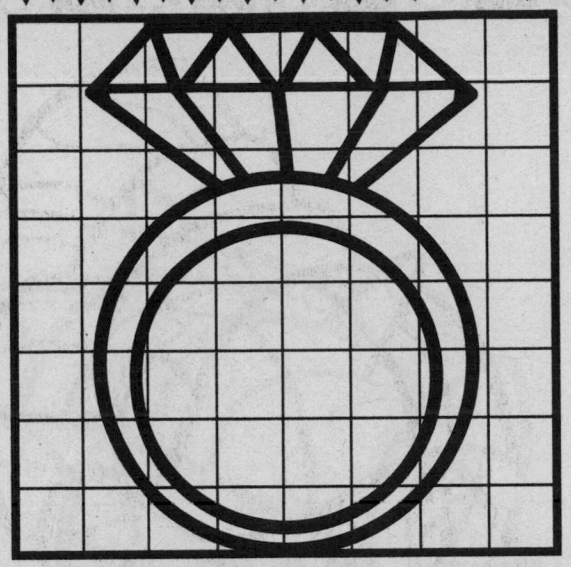

PONY MAZE

Help Spike the Dragon follow the path of stars to Twilight Sparkle.

pony
pals

HOW MANY?

Count the items below and place your answer on the line.

_____ HORSESHOES.

Answer: 5 Horseshoes.

LET'S DRAW!

Rainbow Dash loves to fly!
Draw some rainbows.

to Pinkie

MAKE A MATCH

Look at the 3 ponies in each column. Find the ponies that match and draw a line connecting the two.

SPIKE
THE DRAGON